Locking

Horns

With THE

Federal

(Postal service)

EEO

To order additional copies of this book, contact:
Xlibris Corporation
1-888-795-4274
www.Xlibris.com
Orders@Xlibris.com
55443

Contents

Preface

I have laid this publication in print filled with knowledge of personal experiences and I advise all those who read this to take heed that this is my experience and opinion. I have formed this as best I can in laymen terms and have shared first hand experiences to help provide an inside understanding that you—the reader—will take and utilize as best you can for your own personal battle. Additionally, I suggest you take time to search the internet for as much possible information you can obtain.

I have worked for the Postal Service since February 1986 and have seen several changes over the years—though some unwelcome. I have served as a union steward and a union editor over a 5-year span, along with, being a 204b for an additional 3 years. Thus, I have personally experienced both sides of the force.

I have enjoyed my job as both, letter carrier and 204b. I took pride in my work and have received letters of recommendation from Postmasters, a station manager, a fellow supervisor and several craft employees. I did my job, as a 204b, with the belief and integrity that everyone had the right to go to work, do their job and go home at nights without the worry of someone scrutinizing their every move. I went home at nights and could look at myself in the mirror and know I did my best to maintain my integrity throughout my work day. I demonstrated that the supervisor job within the Postal Service could be done without losing any personal integrity or having to fabricate any stories to manipulate the employees. However, it took only one egotistical "watch me make a name for myself" OIC to change all that and enter me into the world of EEO madness.

Since, May 2007, I have endured several EEO processes in which I have encountered several obstacles that are not, or at best obscurely, explained in any manual or online site that I have found; therefore, I decided to put this booklet together to assist those who are or will be suffering the same mass confusion within the Postal Services' EEO administrative process.

Besides dealing with a process that is a one of a kind—sponsored by the very company that has allegedly violated your rights and yet it is attempting to give the impression they are on your side helping you resolve a situation—you are learning new forms, timeframes and using words not utilized in your daily lives. This can be mind-boggling!

I want you to take your time and read this booklet thoroughly at a pace that allows you to comprehend it. Whether you're someone who can speed-read or takes hours before turning the page—it doesn't matter, just as long as you can comprehend it.

Furthermore, I suggest you get prepared for a very long haul. If you have suffered a demotion or have been placed in a position where you have incurred a financial decrease then I strongly suggest you make preparations and budget for at least a 9-12 month time frame per complaint. The Postal Service has allocated their EEO system enough time for a woman to conceive and give birth twice if the EEO process is taken to the full measure. Add the initial 45 days to make the complaint, with 10 days to reply to the initial packet sent, with the 30 calendar days for informal (90 days if you agree to REDRESS) with the 180 days for formal investigation (270 days if you agree to allocating more time for this investigation or 360 days if you amend a complaint or have multiple complaints to investigate during this stage), with the 30 days to file after receiving the formal investigative report; thereby, giving you a maximum time—until you can either appeal for a decision, a hearing by a judge or go to civil court—a total of 535 days! Remember, that is without having a final decision, a hearing or pursuing a civil suit; thus, you aren't finished yet!

I am neither an attorney nor an EEO advocate and make no pretext of such. I am a union member that has been—in my opinion—discriminated against and harassed beyond legal bounds; therefore, I have filed several EEO complaints and have suffered one obstacle after another with the lack of any guiding hands to ease the stress of sending which documents where or when. Thus again, my decision to putting out this booklet to help those that have been, are now or will be in the same lost predicament as I have been. I do not claim this publication as an all encompassing or currently updated document—as seemingly (if you know the federal government), everything changes within minutes! However, I do believe that, foregoing a major overhaul of the system, this publication will strongly assist anyone to understand and deal emotionally with this process for years to come.

The battle with the EEO administrative procedures is that it has a disorganized and vague set of documents, no one actually on your side that can or will direct you step by step—without costing you extensively and governing laws that are found here and there. However, if you stay focused and have a little insight then you can do it. I will attempt to walk you through this, share with you some experiences, give you some insights, remind you again and again to watch your time frames and try to make as much sense out of this as possible. So read it, set it next to your paperwork as you go along, and read it again as you so need. I hope it helps you, as much as I am praying it will.

First of all—get a calendar and put it up in plain sight so everyday you will look at it and see the time frame for each stage of this complaint process. To help, then highlight this information also. You have to be aware of your days available before reaching a deadline so you can schedule in whatever meetings needed with your representative prior to those dates.

**You are not allowed a grace period—You will notice, that for the most part, the time frames are printed in BOLD letters; yet, there are others where the time frame or an important issue is in the small print. Therefore read every document carefully. **

Time frames and deadlines are on the side of the Postal Service—They are not your friends!

You must proceed with the EEO process in a mind frame that:

- You are NOT in a hurry
- These people are NOT your friends
- You are fighting for YOUR rights
- YOU will be very thorough
- You will mark your TIMEFRAMES

Laws and Publications

There are several laws and publications to assist you in determining which claim to file; however, the biggest obstacle is finding those items. Each of these laws provides much more than I can put into a small helping guidebook; however, I have provided what I deem most helpful for you at this point. Be sure to view these regulations in whole if you feel more information is needed for your case. Remember, this booklet is for a helping hand NOT a complete book with ALL the answers or explicit duplication of other books, laws or manuals.

Remember, it is easy to become frustrated and tired of the hassle but keep telling yourself that YOU are fighting for YOUR rights!

EL-603—This handbook was the last item I found online when searching for a postal form number. I found this helpful and enlightening; however, it is written by the company for the company and (in my opinion) the language takes some interpretation. If you can print this off or use it as a side-help online you won't regret it. It amazes me that this handbook is not offered to employees in the original packet rather than the Publication 133 since it is more in depth and precise. But, then again, maybe that is why it isn't. The Postal Service is governed by Federal laws and abides within them as far as the paperwork is concerned; however, just because they have the handbooks and guidelines don't mean they have to let employees know. I have worked for the Postal Service over 20 years, been a union steward for several years, and worked as a 204b for 3 years; yet, I had never heard of the this handbook until I accidentally bumped into it online!

Publication 133—this pamphlet should be included in the initial packet you receive from the EEO Complaint Office once you have filed your initial complaint whether via personally, on the phone, or mail. Read it thoroughly!

Civil Rights Act of 1991—provides monetary damages of up to $300,000.00 in cases of proven intentional employment discrimination.

Title VII of the Civil Rights Act of 1964, *as amended*—(paraphrased) Title VII prohibits discrimination based on race, color, religion, sex, and national origin. Additionally, it prohibits reprisal/retaliation for taking part in the EEO process and/or opposing ANY unlawful employment practice under its authority.

>>> You can read this on the Internet at www.eeoc.gov/policy/**vii**.html.

Age Discrimination in Employment Act of 1967, *as amended*—(paraphrased) Age discrimination in employment act of 1967 (ADEA) prohibits discrimination in employment based on age (40 years or older). This EEO complaint can be filed directly to a civil action! You are not obligated to pursue this through the EEO process.

However, there are, of course, proper procedures to follow in doing so.

- Before filing your civil suit—YOU MUST file a notice with intent to sue with the Office of Federal Operations, Equal Employment Opportunity Commission.
- YOU MUST file this notice within 180 calendar days of the date of the alleged discriminatory action.
- YOU MUST WAIT 30 calendar days before filing the civil action after you have filed your timely notice of intent to sue.

If you so chose to proceed with the EEO complaint, then you are obligated under Title 29 Code of Federal Regulations part 1614 to exhaust all your administrative remedies prior to filing a civil action.

>>> You can read this on the Internet at www.eeoc.gov/policy/adea.html

** *Notice of intent to sue must be dated and contain the following:*

1. Statement of intent to file a civil action under section 15(d) of the Age Discrimination in Employment Act of 1967, as amended.
2. Your name, address, and telephone number.
3. Name, address, and telephone number of your designated representative, if any.

4. Name and location of the Postal facility where the alleged discriminatory action occurred.
5. Date on which the alleged discriminatory action occurred.
6. Statement of the nature of the alleged discriminatory action(s)
7. Your signature or your representative's signature.

Rehabilitation Act of 1973, *as amended*—(paraphrased) this act is commonly mistaken as the American with Disabilities Act; however, it is not the same! If you are a federal employee you CANNOT file under the ADA. You HAVE to reference the Sections 501 or 505 of the Rehabilitation Act of 1973, as amended. Though these laws are very similar they vary in how you have to enforce your rights.

>>> You can read it on the Internet at http://www.eeoc.gov/policy/rehab.html.

In a disability case it is YOUR burden of responsibility to prove that you:

- Have a disability—The definition of a person with a disability under Section 501 is basically the same as the definition under the Americans with Disabilities Act (ADA).
- Have the required qualifications for the job
- Can perform the "essential functions" of the job—though some reasonable accommodations may be needed.
- That you were discriminated against due to your disability

** Note ** *its not that you need to show they discriminated against you **ONLY** because of your disability; but, that there is a connection between your employer's action **AND** your disability.*

- That the employer failed to make a reasonable accommodation.

** Note ** If the agency can prove that it would impose an "undue hardship" then no accommodation need be given.

Title 29 CFR (part 1614)—FEDERAL SECTOR EQUAL EMPLOYMENT OPPORTUNITY—governs the processing of federal employees discrimination complaints. Section 1614.103 Complaints of discrimination covered by this part. (a) Individual and class complaints of employment discrimination and Retaliation prohibited by title VII (discrimination on the basis of race, color, religion, sex and national origin), the ADEA (discrimination on the basis of age when the aggrieved individual is at least 40 years of age), the Rehabilitation Act (discrimination on the basis of handicap) or the Equal Pay Act (sex-based wage discrimination) shall be processed in accordance with this part. Complaints alleging retaliation prohibited by these statutes are considered to be complaints of discrimination for purposes of this part.

(b) This part applies to:

(1) Military departments as defined in 5 U.S.C. 102;
(2) Executive agencies as defined in 5 U.S.C. 105;
(3) The **United States Postal Service**, Postal Rate Commission and Tennessee Valley Authority;
(4) All units of the judicial branch of the Federal government having positions in the competitive service, except for complaints under the Rehabilitation Act;
(5) The National Oceanic and Atmospheric Administration Commissioned Corps;
(6) The Government Printing Office; and
(7) The Smithsonian Institution.

>>> This is accessible on the Internet at *http://www.eeoc.gov/federal/1614-final.html.*

To be of particular interest is the section 301:

Section 1614.301 (Relationship to Negotiated Grievance Procedure) provides as follows:

(a) When a person is employed by an agency subject to 5 U.S.C. 7121(d) and is covered by a collective bargaining agreement that permits claims of discrimination to be raised in a negotiated grievance procedure, a person wishing to file a complaint or a grievance on a claim of alleged employment discrimination **must elect** to raise the claim under either Part 1614 or the negotiated grievance procedure, **but not both**. An election to proceed under this part is indicated only by the filing of a written complaint; use of the pre-complaint process as described in 1614.105 does not constitute an election

4

for purposes of this section. An aggrieved employee who files a complaint under this part may not thereafter file a grievance on the same claim. An election to proceed under a negotiated grievance procedure is indicated by the filing of a timely written grievance. An aggrieved employee who files a grievance with an agency whose negotiated agreement permits the acceptance of grievances which allege discrimination may not thereafter file a complaint on the same claim under Part 1614 are regardless of whether the agency has informed the individual of the need to elect or of whether the grievance has raised an issue of discrimination. Any such complaint filed after a grievance has been filed on the same claim shall be dismissed without prejudice to the complainant's right to proceed through the negotiated grievance procedure, including the right to appeal to the Commission from a final decision as provided in subpart D of this part. The notice of final action dismissing such a complaint shall advise the complainant of the obligation to raise discrimination in the grievance process and of the right to appeal the final grievance decision to the Commission.

For clarity: This means that you have to chose between filing a grievance through the negotiation process or filing an EEO complaint—you cannot do both!

Equal Pay Act of 1963, *as amended*—(EPA) prohibits sex-based wage discrimination.

>>> This is can be read on the Internet at *www.eeoc.gov/policy/eps.html*

Management Directive MD-110: This is the EEOC management directive and covers all the issues—I don't believe many of these issues are not divulged completely on the EEO.gov website.

I did find a website that offers Postal Employees contact to an EEO advocate at PostalEmployeeadvocate.com so give it a look over and decide if that is best for you.

Educate yourself as much as you possibly can concerning this process—it is tricky and laid with all sorts of fine print and traps to lay your complaint aside for the greater power of the Postal Service.

Here is a glimpse of SOME of your paperwork to come!

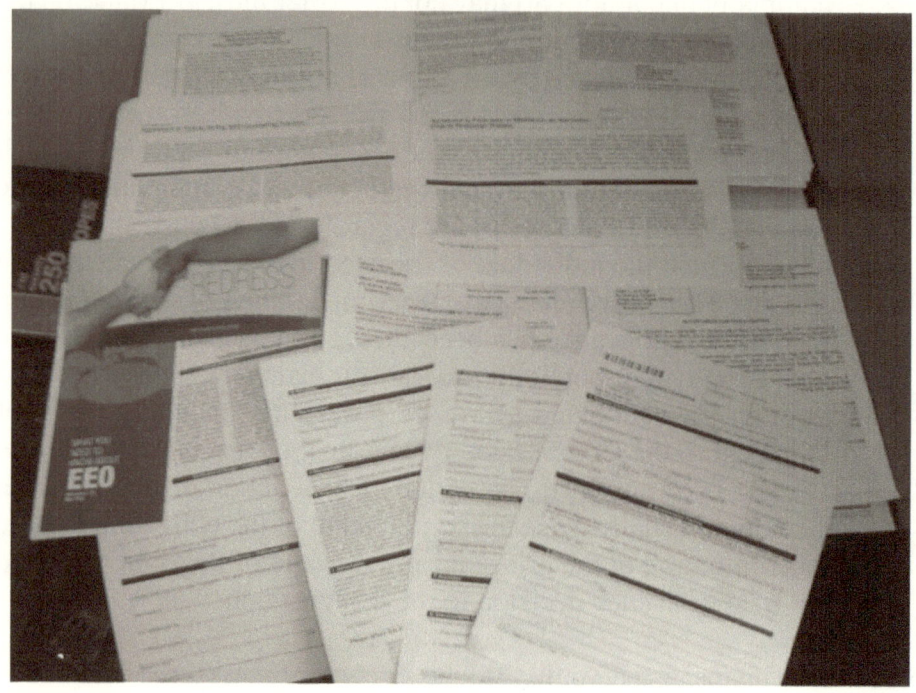

Clean off a table or an area that you can spread these out and work without interruptions. There is a lot being thrown at you all at once and you have a time frame to deal with them!

Stay Focused!

Best Wishes,

LK Cuttill

Chapter 1
Getting Started

(The Informal Stage)

To begin your episode with the EEO administrative process—after you have decided which of your rights have been violated you can either:

Contact:

Your local EEO office personally

Or call the:

National Contact Center at 1-888-EEO-USPS (1-800-336-8777)

For Deaf and hard hearing call:

National Contact Center at 1-800-877-8339

Or you can write to:

EEO Complaint Processing
US Postal Service
475 L'Enfant Plaza SW
Washington DC 20260-4135

This will start your pre-complaint process with a Dispute Resolution Specialist (DRS). You **MUST** make this contact within *45 calendar days of the incident* you believe to have been discriminatory and caused the alleged violation *OR* if it was a personnel action, then you **MUST** make this contact within *45 days of the effective date of the action*.

You don't have to rush out and contact them within a few days so attempt to resolve it yourself (take notes whenever you meet with anyone) at each level above you.

I went directly to my supervisor, station manager, postmaster and POOM; however, I didn't get any resolve. Thus, I started writing letters to the District manager, Area manager and ended up sending letters to the Postmaster General and several politicians. I still didn't get any resolution. Although, I built a strong case to show that I attempted every possible means to resolve it. Therefore, the hard look is now upon them if/when it goes to civil court as to why they knew from front line supervisor to the very top guy; yet, never attempted to resolve it within.

A very important point for you to remember is that you need to put the bad eye upon the company at every possible chance you get—remember this is a fight! So don't step back when you could be stepping in for a knock out punch.

Keep all your documents in a file—organized for later usage—as all of this will assist your complaint later in the formal EEO process and (if needed) Civil court. But remember to mark your calendar so you do not miss the 45-day mark.

Also, at this time you should sit down and make a chronological order list for everything that has transpired since you first noticed you were being discriminated against. Add every thing that happens to this list daily to keep it accurate. It will save you a lot of time trying to remember something later! Every letter sent, every person talked with, every event or happening—it all goes onto this list. When you send paperwork to anyone—you need to be sure to send it priority mail with delivery confirmation or certified so you can print out the track and confirm and staple it to the receipt and then staple that to your folder.

I searched the Internet for as much information as I could collect and I read the Guidebook of Laws and Programs for People with Disabilities, EL-603, Publication 133, the ADA—before I found out that it didn't apply to federal employees, and the 501 of the Rehabilitation Act of 1973 several times while getting my focus for the several EEO complaints I filed in 2007.

You will receive an initial packet from the EEO Field Programs manager providing you with an acknowledgement letter, a PS Form 2564-A, (Information for Pre-Complaint Counseling)—that **MUST** be returned to them within 10 calendar days, a PS Form 2567-A, (An agreement to extend 30-day counseling), a Publication 133, (What you need to know about EEO), a PS Form 2563-A, (Certification of Receipt of the pub 133), a PS Form 2567-B, (Agreement to Participate in REDRESS) and a Publication 94 (REDRESS).

** **Note** ** notice the 2564-A states *10 CALENDAR days*—meaning if Sunday falls as your tenth day and we all know you can't mail on Sundays—well, that's your loss! Make sure you count 10 calendar days and mark a calendar to remind you when it **MUST** be sent back. The EL603 explains the process of calculating the calendar days and notes that if the final day is a Saturday, Sunday or federal holiday then it is moved back to the next business day; however, you must make it a practice to NOT wait until the last day or trust that the DRS has read the EL603. Basically, what I am trying to share with you is that you should not allow any possible reason to disqualify your complaint; especially, something as shallow as missing a time frame. Additionally, there are contradictions from the EL603 and the letters you will receive from the DRS—letters state the 10 calendar days start the date you receive it; however, the EL603 states it starts the day AFTER you receive it. Hence, don't take chances! Count 10 calendar days and mark your calendar accordingly to when you receive it.

This is your initial packet to start your complaint process

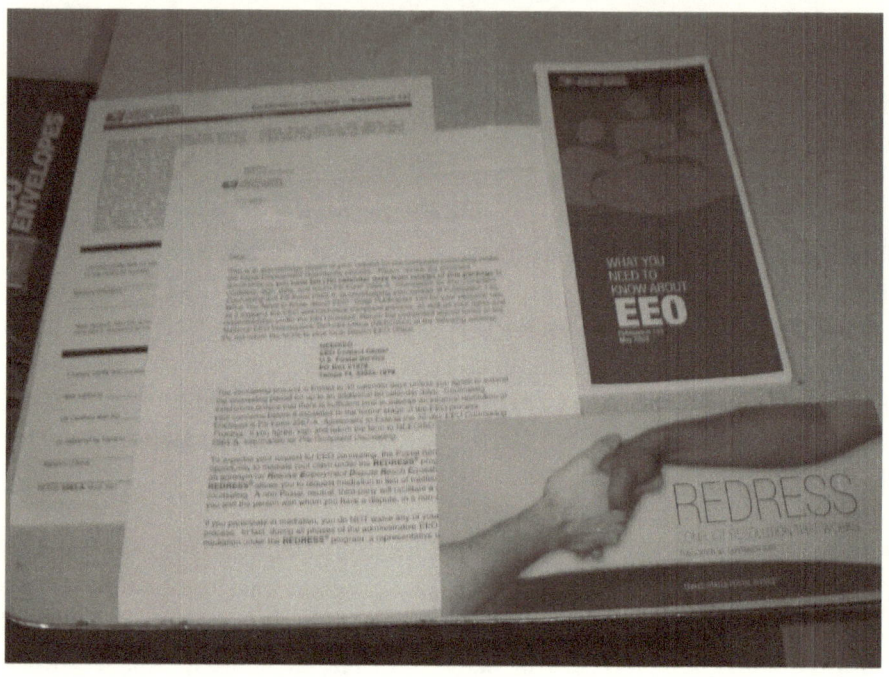

*** Annotate deadlines on your calendar! ***

If you fail to return it within the *10 calendar days of the date you received* it then your complaint will most commonly be closed.

There are exceptions to the time frames during this process; however, to obtain these you must prove:

- You were unaware of the time limitations
- You were unaware of the violation within the 45 day limitation to filing
- You were prevented due to circumstances outside of your control
- You had other sufficient reasoning for making an untimely filing

The EEO compliance and appeals coordinator will make the determination if you have proven your case and may extend the time frame if he/she so desires.

Without causing any delay to the process, you are allowed to pick/designate a representative at any stage of the process. You can change representatives at any time; as long as you inform the EEO representative and you do not cause any delay at whatever stage your complaint is in.

If your representative is another postal employee then you will be allowed and can expect a reasonable amount of official time to present the complaint and to respond to information requests by the agency during normal work hours. Reasonable amount of time will vary from case to case on any portion of an hour to hours. Advance approval from the immediate supervisor is a **MUST** to obtain the amount of reasonable official time. Due to the critical time frame in responding at each stage of this administrative process a grievance has been won in Decatur, Illinois to provide language that locks a 3-4 day maximum delay for management to allow the reasonable time with your representative. The sooner the better; however, due to service issues immediate time allocation is not always available.

Complainants and their designated representatives are allowed to attend EEO meetings and hearings while on official time if so required; however, they **MUST** present the requests in writing to their immediate supervisor prior to the scheduled meetings/hearings.

The 2564-A

Above Section A there is an important message in small print! *"This is the only notification that you will receive regarding the necessity for you to complete this form."* Now does this sound like a company willing to resolve complaints or attempt to slide them under the carpet? This important factor is in SMALL print!

Section A—Is all information about yourself and pretty self-explanatory.

Section B—You must state the discrimination factors—meaning you have to declare which law was violated. Sex, Age (40+), race, color, religion, national origin, disability or retaliation and you must be specific about it; otherwise you leave it to the discretion of the DRS and take the risk of having it closed for lack of information or some other catch 21 they can come up with to dissolve the complaint. Read the laws I have listed in the front and if you are still not sure then go online and read them more specifically for better details.

The lower section of section B is for retaliation allegations and if your complaint is filed prior to getting the case number for the initial complaint state so in the blank for the case number. You know the dates of the initial alleged violation so put that in and annotate something to indicate "no number assigned as of this date" in the blank for case number.

Section C—You only have a few lines to describe the violation in this section so be brief; however, be accurate! Outline it if necessary but be to the point so that your DRS will not have to play guessing games because they won't—you will lose out and case closed.

Section D—Comparisons are needed in this section so be mindful of what is going on in your area. Talk with others to see if anyone is aware of similar or conflicting treatment of others in a similar situation as your case. Once again, you can see there are few lines for your information so you need to be direct and condensed.

Section E—Indicate which officials are responsible for the alleged violations. There is room for only two responsible officials; however, you can add more on a piece of paper and refer to this section. Remember to refer to each of these individuals on every document that you sign during this complaint process. I am not saying that the EEO department would intentionally remove people from the case; however, keep in mind these people are Postal paid employees and they are (at least in my area) housed within the same building as our Area managers; hence, they work, have daily dialogue with and could even have lunch with those you have charged. At times, these are the individuals that could have stopped or resolved your claim within days of the alleged violation if they so desired to. I, personally, believe that higher level Postal Service managers have an ostrich style of managing—turn their backs to you and stick their heads in a hole in hopes it will all go away! Therefore, I suggest you always be attentive to your paperwork and be specific with those named as charged.

The lower section of section E refers to the retaliation allegations and once again, you can see there is limited space to write. So be precise in your writings.

Section F—Asks for the resolution you are seeking and I cannot impress upon you strong enough to be careful of what you ask for.

Here is a list of proper remedies that can be obtained through an EEO complaint:

1. You can have a notice to ALL employees of the violating agency of their right to be free from discrimination *ALONG* with a promise from the agency that this particular discrimination, they were found guilty of, would not happen again.
2. You can receive a commitment from the agency that it will cease engaging in said discrimination and commit to taking whatever action needed to ensure it never happens again.
3. You can get an unconditional offer to put you in the position you should have been—or one equal to—had the discrimination never occurred.
4. You can get any loss wages suffered from the discriminatory action. **Make a note here—if you do not request compensatory damages at the informal or formal stages then you cannot ask for it later at the hearing or settlement negotiations.**
5. You can receive any other monetary loss you suffered related to the discrimination.

Section G—Here you are questioned if you have already filed a grievance or a MSPB appeal on this same issue—self-explanatory.

You will receive a PS Form 2567-B that gives you the option to agree to participate in REDRESS. Give thought to this, as it can be a positive aspect if both parties act favorably and in good faith; however, this is a leap of faith. Additionally, you could use this opportunity to see what factors they are relying upon that you were unaware of. At one of my REDRESS meetings the manager provided a document totally altered from the one I had originally provided and openly admitted giving documentation that is governed by regulations to have been given elsewhere; thereby, strengthening my argument while at the same time giving me insight to their commitment to winning this complaint to the extent of doctoring paperwork. So, I support REDRESS for the purpose of obtaining knowledge and insight to management's angle taken to repress the complaint. REDRESS meetings are done ON the clock with the named postal managers (that you named on your PS Form 2654-A) and a professionally trained mediator (who is NOT a postal employee but is paid by the Postal Service). If you agree in writing to participate in REDRESS then your process period is **90 calendar days from the date of your request for EEO counseling**.

** **Note**—not all issues are REDRESS appropriate. Your EEO counselor will advise you if such is the case. **

Regardless of issues addressed in REDRESS if your complaint continues on to the formal stage after the 90 calendar days then *ONLY* the issues you included in your PS Form 2564-A will be included in the formal complaint.

You will receive a PS Form 2563-A, which is nothing more than a certification of receipt of the publication 133. This publication is very helpful; however, it is disorganized and vague in several areas—at least to me it was.

The PS Form 2567-A, (An Agreement to extend 30-day counseling) is provided to allow you to give them permission to take an additional 30 days to attempt to settle your complaint at the informal stage with the DRS. I have no idea why anyone would give a DRS an additional 30 days to do something they couldn't complete in the original time frame and prolong the delay in processing this complaint to the formal investigation to attain the completion of this process as quickly as possible. I feel the Postal Service has allocated enough time to process one complaint—that if done properly and time constraints were placed on the DRS and investigators as equally as they are upon the complainant then the EEO process could have handled several complaints properly. Hence, my opinion that the Postal Service has no—that's right

"NO"—intention of giving your complaint the uninterrupted attention it deserves. But, remember, this is YOUR complaint and your life and rights that you are making decisions on; therefore, do what you feel is right for you.

Send in supporting facts and documents needed to convince the DRS the complaint is valid and requires attention. You are NOT required to send ALL documentation—I suggest that you don't; however, keep in mind that you have to convince the DRS this is a valid complaint. Therefore, you determine what data is pertinent and strong enough to make that convincing statement. The DRS is a counselor and should act appropriately. This individual is NOT your formal investigator; however, he/she will gather information about the jurisdiction issues such as the timeliness of your forms—of which gives the DRS the authority to close your complaint if you are late! The DRS should explain to you the EEO complaint process, REDRESS and any agreeable resolutions possible. The DRS has **thirty days from the date on which you first initiated your request for EEO counseling** to complete or resolve your issue unless you agree to extend the period; of which, this agreement **MUST** be in writing. I do not support delaying your case; however, it is your opinion and your case.

The DRS will review agency regulations, documents and talk with management and craft in an attempt to informally resolve this situation. If this matter is not resolved within the time frame then the DRS *should* conduct a final interview and will issue you a notice of right to file a formal complaint by either certified mail or in person. I underline should because I was never given a final interview on any of my EEO complaints!

In short, the DRS will conduct an informal inquiry and explain to you the EEO process; however for the most part, will not obtain extensive documentation or written testimonies. This is all informal and the DRS should just be considered a go-between middleman—nothing more.

** *Keep in mind, these people are postal employees that are (in my area) housed and work daily at the side of those higher in the company that have violated your rights or have done nothing to resolve your complaints on their own merit; thus, you decide the extent you wish to trust them.* **

Additionally, at this stage you can choose to remain anonymous! I do not know why you would choose this as if they cannot figure it out and when it goes to formal complaint stage you will lose the anonymity anyway.

With my one of my EEO complaints on retaliation I had to file a complaint against the EEO counselor for wrongfully combining all my complaints into one case number and closing them after I withdrew the individual complaint that she filed them all under. So it is worth mentioning here that if you file several complaints and they are referring to the same issue, then more often than not, the counselor will combine them; however, if these several complaints are of different issues they **CANNOT** and **SHOULD NOT** be filed under the same number. More specifically, if the Dispute Resolution Specialist does combine your issues together you should receive notification. Do not accept notification via a phone call! You have no proof to file away for future usage to prove or disprove what was said. Keep in mind once again, if the Postal Service was trustworthy—you would not be in this situation. So be very adamant and clear concerning your complaints with the counselor if they try to combine several together at the informal level. Take note that this is the informal level—rules change at the formal level. If you have several complaints that are accepted at the formal level then this will be combined in to one *INVESTIGATION*. You must comprehend the difference, as it is essential you understand this. Only like issues should be allowed to be combined under the same number. Different complaints for various issues should never be allowed to be combined under the same number! At the formal stage the combination of complaints can be combined under one *INVESTIGATION (not number)*. I won this EEO complaint and all my complaints were reopened to include the one I withdrew at REDRESS. I cannot stress enough that you have to protect your rights—they will not!

This will get you started in the right direction. Just remember to mark a calendar for every stage of the EEO process you are in. Read the forms and letters they send to you carefully—remember the small print!

If you are late returning your packet within the 10-day timeframe you will receive this notification of closing your request.

I have stated before and repeat again—READ through all the paperwork you are sent very carefully!

Cancellation of Request to Initiate EEO Counseling

12/10/2007

Decatur, IL

SUBJECT: Cancellation of Request to Initiate EEO Counseling

Dear I,

I am writing in regard to your request to initiate EEO counseling submitted to the EEO Contact Center on 11/16/2007.

On 11/19/2007, PS Form 2564-A, Information for Pre-complaint Counseling was mailed to yo asking you to provide basic information necessary to initiate the EEO process. The package also indicated that forms not completed and returned within ten (10) calendar days from recei may result in the closing of your EEO contact for failure to proceed.

As of today, you have not returned the requested form or provided the information necessar, begin the processing of your EEO complaint. Your request for counseling is, therefore, close

If you believe that this decision should be reconsidered, please contact the undersigned in writing within (5) days of your receipt of this correspondence.

Sincerely,

Joseph R. Bruce

** *Notice this letter provides you a 5-day timeframe from the date you receive it to request reconsideration*

Chapter 2
REDRESS

THIS IS YOUR REDRESS BOOKLET

I have touched up on this briefly earlier; yet, it bears a bit more detailing, as many will opt to meet at this informal mediated stage.

In the original packet you receive after you initiate your first contact with the EEO complaints processing office you will receive (or should receive) a PS Form 2567-B, Agreement to participate in REDRESS, an alternative dispute resolution process. Read this carefully! Signing this is your voluntary agreement to participate in a mediation process and it extends your pre-complaint processing period from 30 calendar days to 90 calendar days. Weigh your pros and cons before signing this. I agreed to REDRESS on one of my several complaints and was glad I did because I got to see exactly how low down and underhanded these guys were going to play; hence, it gave me heads up to the depth that I would have to secure my paperwork and supporting documents to overcome their unethical standards. Additionally, it led to my filing an EEO complaint against the EEO DRS.

Your DRS will send you a Memorandum/letter when your REDRESS mediation conference is scheduled. It should list the management official, representatives for both sides (if any), yourself, EEO case number (double check it to ensure you are meeting on the right complaint) along with the date and place of the conference. This letter has some very important information so take the time to read all of it! If you do not know what to clock to and your supervisor has not directed you; then check in the M-32 Handbook. To date, operation numbers 630 through 634 have been commonly used and suggested. Additionally, this letter will list the counselee's claim—read this and verify with your DRS if this is the only issue to be addressed.

During one of my REDRESS conferences the letter stated only one claim; however, the DRS had instructed me verbally over during a phone conversation to consider all my complaints involved and discuss whatever issues I deem necessary. Contrarily, the mediator and management had not gotten that message (or just ignored it); therefore, each time I brought up another related topic they would reply "irrelevant" and refuse to discuss it any further.

At this meeting you will meet with the managers you listed on your PS Form 2564-A, a mediator provided by the postal service, and your representative can be present as well. The mediator will give a little speech on what his/her responsibility at this meeting is and is not. All present will be requested to sign an "agreement to mediate" form that will list the guidelines for the voluntary meeting.

I strongly urge you to be direct with your DRS prior to attending this meeting and be 100% clear on what topics you can address and what topics will not be allowed. At my REDRESS I was told one thing by my DRS and had my ideas on what to discuss; however, the management side had a different set of rules; thus, it was a cluster flare!

Remember, REDRESS meetings are done on the clock and can take several hours.

If your meeting is successful and you achieve your remedy—it is not binding until it is in writing! Therefore, do not leave this meeting without the written settlement agreement being signed by all parties required.

Any agreement for settlement MUST be in writing; however, do not get over confident—that doesn't mean they will abide by it. I settled an EEO complaint during a REDRESS; however, within 3 days after making this agreement, it was breached and I had to file a Breach of Settlement statement to reopen the complaint.

Though a breach of settlement is filed, there is no guarantee the complaint will be reopened. The EEO process allows a grace area for the Postal Service. To assist you in understanding this grace area, here are a few examples of what happened to me:

- An agreement stated management would provide written statements posted at each station within a time frame—however, this did not happen. Therefore, I filed a breach of settlement—the EEO agent informed me that it was eventually done; therefore, no damage was suffered.
- An agreement was made and by the second day the confidentiality of the meeting was breached and I had to file a breach of settlement; however, the EEO agent disputed that management has the right to talk amongst one another to carry out the agreement. Hence, no damage was done to me; therefore no damage was done. The managers that disclosed the breach to me were "talked to" and instructed that they were not to share information with craft.

Though these arguments were given to me via phone conversations; eventually, I did receive a letter from the Dispute Resolution Coordinator of the decision that a breach had occurred and was sent the documentation to re-open my EEO complaint to the next stage (meaning I was sent documentation to file a formal complaint since that would be the next step from the informal stage). It should be obvious to you by now that postal management and the EEO counselors will try to manipulate you into closing out your complaint at the earliest stage without giving you anything. You will be misled (I call it lied to) and misinformed via conversations that cannot be proven so, my advice, is to wait until it is written before you react.

Comparatively, if your meeting proves to destroy your stand on your complaint, you have the choice to withdraw your complaint or parts of it. The mediator will provide you with a PS Form 2564-C, Withdrawal of complaint of discrimination that you will need to sign and date. However, be very careful when doing this as it could cost you dearly!

There are two boxes to check mark on this form under the line—"do hereby voluntarily withdraw":

- My request for EEO counseling or formal EEO complaint in its entirety
- The following allegation(s) ONLY
- If you have filed more than one complaint be sure your DRS did not combine them under this one number because if he/she did and your not sure of it when you withdraw this REDRESS complaint in its entirety—then it withdraws the complaints combined under it as well. I firmly recommend you never withdraw a complaint at this meeting! You can withdraw a complaint at any time during an EEO process; therefore, take the time to think over the events at the REDRESS and talk with your DRS to ensure you are only withdrawing that one issue and not any others. Remember, the Dispute Resolution Specialist is a postal paid employee, as is the mediator; therefore, put your trust in only yourself and your representative.

There are no dumb questions in the REDRESS phase; thus, take your documents, notes, presumptions and get answers to everything you can imagine—it can only help you later—even if it is to make a withdrawal. You cannot make an educated judgment if you do not have answers; however, once again, be careful and not be manipulated by lies and deceit. Obtain knowledge of documents and facts that can be checked on after the meeting to confirm their statements and explanations. As I have stated before, you can withdraw anytime during this EEO process so it doesn't have to be done at this meeting.

This meeting is to be held in confidentiality; however, after one of my REDRESS meetings, and the filing of an EEO on the DRS, I received a letter from the district EEO manager, which had statements from the managers and mediator on what they believed had occurred in the meeting.

As you have read prior when management kept saying "irrelevant" and would not discuss the other topic—well, they gave statements to the EEO manager and DRS that they didn't stop me from discussing any issue and that I was given every opportunity possible. On another complaint REDRESS the manager involved at the meeting held training with other managers and used the settlement of the REDRESS as his explanation for the documentation needed; thereby, breaching the confidentiality of the Privacy Act notice that all are required to sign at the REDRESS. Hence, keep in mind that not all things are as management attempts to make you believe.

It will benefit you to keep a mindset that you are in a fight and those smiling in your face at this meeting are the ones that violated your rights without regard to your welfare that created this situation.

Chapter 3

Formal Complaint Stage

At the completion of the informal stage, your DRS *is required to* send you a packet to include a PS Form 2570, (EEO Dispute Resolution Specialist's (DRS) Inquiry Report), a PS Form 2565, (EEO Complaint of Discrimination in the Postal Service), a PS Form 2565-A, (Withdrawal of Formal EEO Complaint of Discrimination) and a 2579-A, (Notice of Right to File Individual Complaint). These will give you guidance to the next step and the forms to proceed with. At this point, you get to read the Dispute Resolution Specialists Inquiry—the final report from the DRS.

Do not get upset! Do not let anything stated in this report take your focus off your complaint. You must continue your vision on civil court and stay determined in your endeavor to retain documentation to secure a favorable decision while this case continues through the required EEO administration process. Do not let yourself believe you have lost from the decision made by this Postal Employee that works in this position to stave off complaints and protect the service.

Focus on this as if your preparing for a civil court case—do not give birth to any belief that there will be a resolution in your favor under this process—a process set up by the very company that has violated YOUR rights. If your case is strong enough to warrant a Postal employee determining that there is no defense for the company at the informal stage then you would have been offered a settlement prior to this point; therefore, you should be expecting negativity in this DRS inquiry. So don't lose your FOCUS!

OK, now we are at the Formal Stage!

Once you have decided to continue with the Formal Complaint stage you need to:

- Fill out the PS Form 2565
- Be explicit since you do not send supporting documentation with this
- Return no later than 15 days AFTER receiving the notice of right to file to be considered timely
- Postal service recommends—not requires—but, recommends the complainant send a copy of the formal complaint to the DRS. I do not know why nor would I recommend it; however, if your buddies with your DRS and feel comfortable with it—then as I have stated before, it is your complaint.

Your complaint must include:

- Your name
- Address
- Phone number
- Social security number
- Your title and position (if you are an applicant then it must be stated as well)
- Name and title of official(s) responsible for the alleged violation
- Name of the postal facility where it allegedly occurred
- Date of incident
- Exactly what violation/discrimination it was that caused the complaint
- Explicit description of the allegations
- Date you received your 2579-A, (notice of right to file an individual complaint)
- Name of DRS
- Whether a grievance had been initiated or filed—or a MSPB appeal filed (include the dates of either if applicable)
- If you have a representative then include:

- o Name
- o Title
- o Business/residential (if not a businessman/attorney) address
- o Phone number

Be sure to sign and date your complaint—if you have an attorney, he/she must sign and date it.

You will receive a notification from the EEO compliance and appeals coordinator or a designee of ***acknowledgement of your complaint*** and then another notification later to inform you whether your complaint(s) have been ***accepted for investigation*** (or dismissed) in whole or partially.

To be accepted for investigation a complaint must have these 4 characteristics:

- It must be jurisdictional founded—meaning, an aggrieved applicant for employment or an employee for a specific claim of discrimination must file it.
- MUST be filed in a timely manner
- MUST be filed with the designated EEO complaints processing office
- MUST be specific and detailed

** Note ** If you are filing a complaint with other individuals concerning a similar incident—the EEO coordinator may combine all of these into one complaint. He/she must inform you of this consolidation!

Formal Complaint Acknowledgements
And Acceptance Letters

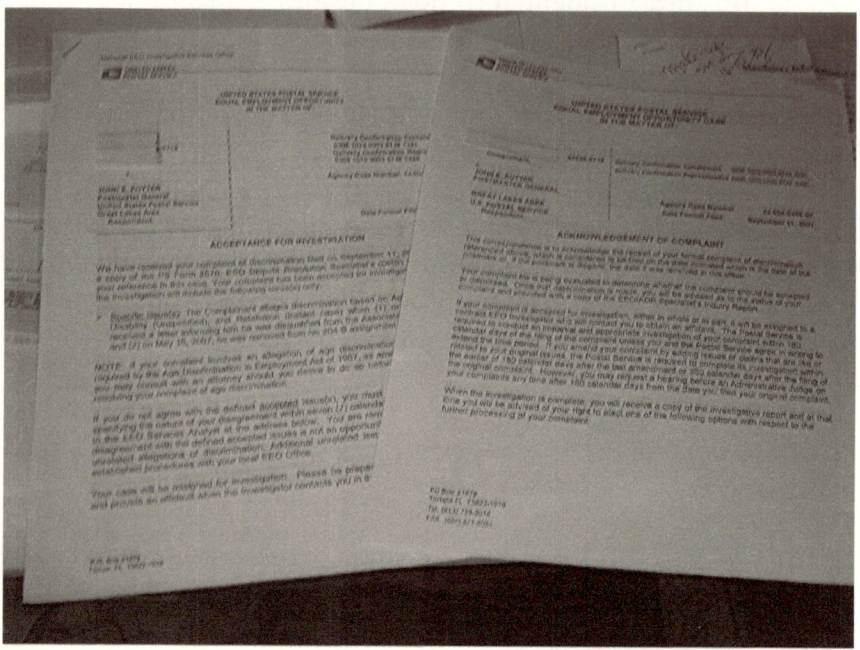

** *You will receive a formal Acknowledgement of Complaint document that will inform you of their receipt of your complaint and that they will determine if your complaint will be accepted in whole or partially.*

** *You will receive a formal Acceptance for Investigation document if your complaint is accepted in whole or partially—this letter will explicitly describe which item(s) are accepted and which are not (if any).*

** *I cannot express strong enough for you to read these thoroughly!* **

The dismissal of a complaint is a final agency decision thus can take up to the full 180 days allocation. This dismissal letter must be sent to you via certified mail. You will be notified of your appeal rights within this letter—so read it carefully. Additionally, this letter MUST inform you that if you appeal this to the EEOC's Office of Federal Operations then **you MUST** also send a copy of this appeal and its supporting documentation to the EEO compliance and appeals coordinator! You must appeal within 30 days of your receipt of the decision or you may file a civil suit within

90 days of the receipt. If an attorney represents you then the timeline is started when the attorney receives the decision.

Partial dismissals must be sent to you via certified mail and the letter must acknowledge the receipt of your compliant, list the issues accepted and those dismissed, reasons for supporting the dismissals and explain your appeal rights. An EEOC Form 573 will be attached to your letter. You may appeal the partial dismissals.

Soon following the notification of acceptance you will receive a letter from the EEO manager assigning your case to a formal investigator. Don't think this will be within a few days—remember they are in no hurry since the Postal Service has allotted them ample time. For instance, one of my complaints was given a formal date filed as September 11, 2007; however, I didn't receive the letter assigning it to an investigator until the first week of October 2007. Furthermore, I didn't receive any contact from the investigator until the final days of October! Hence from the formal filing date to the time I was contacted by the investigator was a loss of 46 days. They are in no hurry!

When a complaint is accepted for the formal stage it is typical for the DRS to be assigned as the investigator since he/she already has current knowledge of the complaint. Though, it is not mandatory to do so. I have never had this happen; therefore, I am not sure how often it does happen. However, I filed an EEO against my DRS on one of my complaints; thus, making it good sense to assign it elsewhere. My formal investigator was located in Nebraska so I had to be very explicit on my charges, names of those involved, their positions, their responsibilities and the locations since he, obviously, had no knowledge of our facility and its operations. You should take it into consideration while filling out your forms that you are trying to convince someone totally ignorant of the Postal Service as a whole; thereby, being very explicit and over analytical on each incident to give them a clear vision of your complaint. Anything less would only hamper your cause.

The investigator will send you a letter annotating the charges he will be investigating, the questions he needs answered separately and fully in writing under oath, PS Form 2571, the forms to be used (PS Form 2568-A, EEO Investigative Affidavit and the PS F 2569, Affidavit Continuation Sheets) and requesting that you put your answers in a narrative format.

You have 15 days to return these forms with all questions thoroughly and explicitly answered. Keep in mind as you are filling out your answers that this investigator does not know you nor of the event your alleging caused the discrimination so provide extensive details to give him/her a foundation to disprove. You have the BURDEN to prove your case. This individual will gather information based on the details you provide him of the incident and prepares an investigation file for all involved. The investigator does not make a judgment! He/she **ONLY** gathers information directly involved and related to the details you provide at this point of the incident. Your goal at this point is to direct his investigation into the matters directly related to the alleged discrimination/ incident to achieve the result that you are searching for.

Furthermore, while you are writing your responses DO NOT make derogatory remarks about an individual or be aggressive towards anyone since by all legal definition your complaint is against the Postal Service as a whole—not an individual. Frequently remind yourself of this if need be. Don't let it appear you are headhunting, because then you are viewed as the violator rather than having the appearance of a victim.

You will feel as though you have waited a lifetime before getting any further information; however, they do have a timeframe and in most cases they are timely. Upon the completion of the investigation the file will be turned over to the EEO complaints processing specialist, of whom, will review the case. The specialist, if the case is strong and deems an immediate settlement could be donned, will provide the PCES executive—who has the authority to make a settlement for the area in which the complaint was initiated—with a copy of the investigative file, a copy of Form 2565-D, Notification of Completed Investigation, and a blank copy of Form 2565-B, EEO Settlement Agreement. The PCES executive has 15 days to determine whether or not to resolve this case. Mediation could be arranged for the parties to negotiate the settlement. This is within the 180-day original time frame. If a resolution is attained it MUST be in writing and both parties get a copy of it. If no resolution is obtained then the EEO compliance and appeals coordinator or senior EEO complaints processing specialist will augment the file with Form 2565-D, Notification of Completed Investigation, and provide a copy of the investigative file to the complainant and his/her representative accompanied with a letter explaining your rights of appeal.

You have 30 days after receipt of this investigative file to request a hearing before an administrative judge or a final agency decision without a hearing.

*** Note ** If you do not get a response from the EEO complaints processing specialist and the 180 day timeframe has elapsed then you may request a hearing or final agency decision at will. ***

Your Investigative File

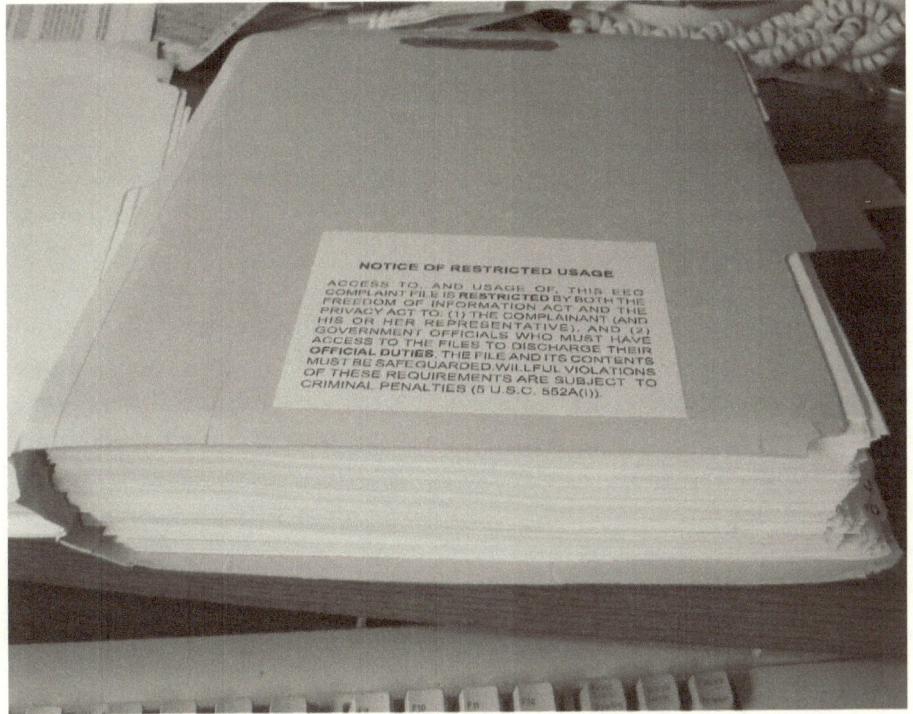

To request the EEOC hearing you must send your request directly to the EEOC district office *AND* a copy of the request to the Postal Service NEEOISO office *AT THE SAME TIME*. The EEO appeals processing center will issue a letter to the EEOC district office, in which the complaint was initiated, to request an administrative judge be appointed. You will receive a copy of this letter, so read it carefully and file it in your folder for later referral if needed.

Chapter 4
EEO Hearing

***It is at this stage that I strongly suggest you
retain an attorney!***

Remember the old saying:

> *"If you choose to be your own attorney, then you have
> a fool for a client!"*

I have advised you as best I can; regardless of the fact, that I used a fellow co-worker as my representative through the entire process. I had a very open and shut case that would embarrass several postal managers if it were to proceed to civil court; hence, I refused to forfeit a percentage of my monetary awards to pay for an attorney. I read and re-read all documents, laws, publications and investigative files to keep my mind focused on every aspect of this case throughout the entire process. I was working on angles and getting statements while the Formal Investigator was working on getting his affidavits. Time is the strongest working factor that the EEO process uses and it is the one the Postal Service counts on to weed out many complaints.

If you do not keep records of every occurrence nor annotate notes daily as you proceed through this process then you have a huge percentage rate of forgetting important issues on the case; thereby, weakening your possibility of succeeding with a positive resolution.

The first page of the investigative file will be the **Transmittal of Investigative File** page containing your rights to appeal a hearing or a decision and it includes the addresses to be contacted.

I know I repeat myself throughout this book; however, it is necessary to keep you focused—***READ THIS FILE THOROUGHLY!***

Transmittal Page

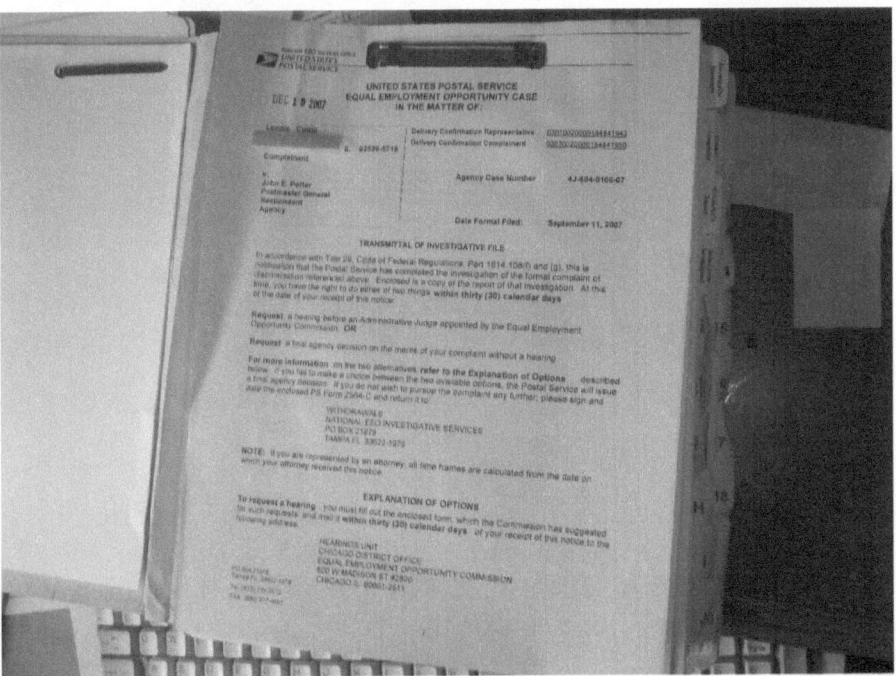

This file can at times be very large; however, it is your EEO cases, with your rights at risk, so don't be hesitant to grab a cup of coffee and some quiet time to read everything therein.

My latest investigative file size

Within this file you will also receive the form requested by the Commission to be used for such requests for a hearing. This form *MUST* be mailed within (30) thirty calendar days of your receipt. If you already have an attorney then it is based upon the time he/she receives the investigative file.

If you do nothing at all then the Postal Service will issue you a final agency decision; thereby, you will lose your right to a hearing altogether.

The form requesting a hearing

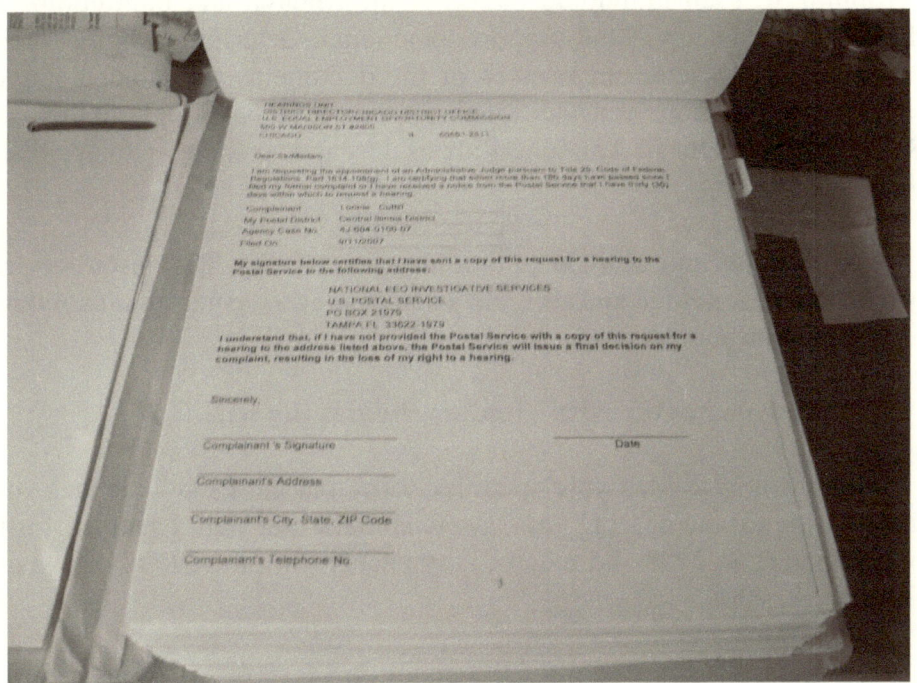

Additionally within this packet is the PS Form 2564-C, Withdrawal of Complaint of Discrimination; therefore, if you feel the case file proves beyond a shadow of a doubt that you will lose then you simply fill this form out and mail it in.

Do not rush to make this decision—REMEMBER, this is their case investigation; therefore, it will be dressed to elude several factors. Thus, you will need to pick this file apart and find all the supporting factors hidden within prior to making an immediate decision to withdraw.

I simplified the task by breaking apart this file into several folders pertaining to each individual that gave an affidavit and then combing through each statement and support document to determine whether their affidavits contradicted themselves or the documents available. I found several contradictions and additional supporting facts throughout the file. So, keep in mind that not all things are as they appear so dig in to decipher your case file.

** Give some serious thought to retaining an attorney. The postal service will be well represented and they will attempt in every aspect to manipulate and intimidate you. **

EEO advocates do exist—finding them is the trick!

Once you have filed your specified form that the EEOC dictates you use in filing for the hearing you have to sit back and wait. I sent my form in on January 4, 2008 and received my packet from the EEOC Judge on February 8, 2008.

If you recall, I started my EEO claim on May 16th, 2007 and finally an EEOC judge acknowledged it on February 8, 2008. As I have stated before—THEY ARE IN NO HURRY!

Within this Acknowledgement and Scheduling Order you will be directed on how the proceedings of the case will be until the actual hearing is completed.

READ THIS THOROUGHLY!!

MARK YOUR CALENDAR!!!

HIGHLIGHT THE SECTIONS OF THE ORDER THAT HAS DATES AND SPECIFIC GUIDELINES!!!!

From here out this is your bible of rules so you must be very conscientious on specifics and fulfilling the requests made by the judge otherwise he has the authority to dismiss your claim.

At this time you need to resubmit your choice of a representative or whether you have chosen to proceed without one. A form will be provided for you to check mark the box preceding the choice you make and requires a signature.

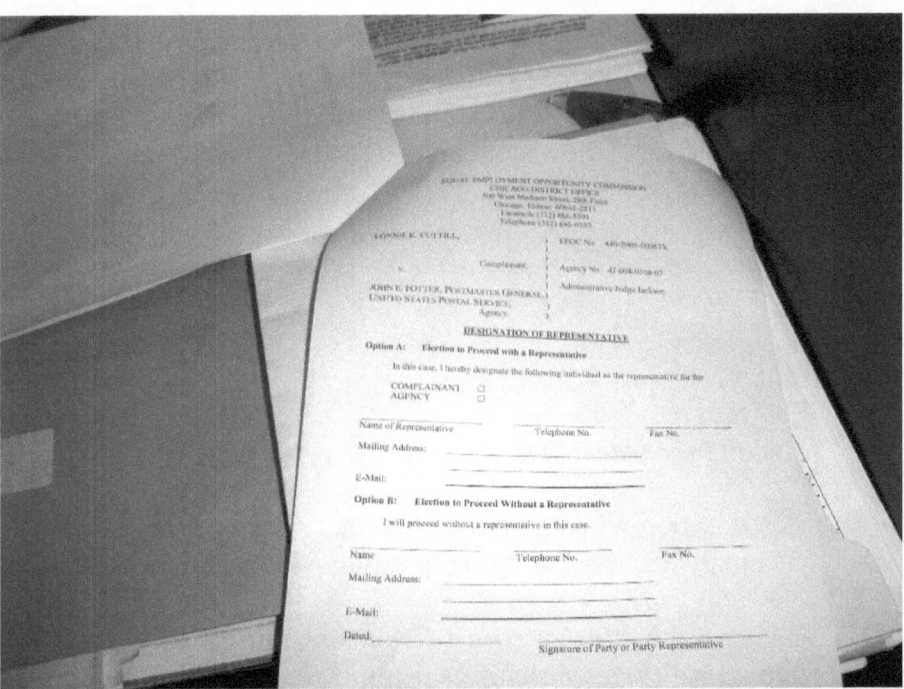

Check mark the choice and fill in the information

The next section should be encouraging the parties to contact one another to initiate attempt to resolve and a number of calendar days will be allocated. If an agreement is reached the agency MUST submit a copy of this settlement in writing to the judge.

Discovery is the most interesting and sometimes confusing segment of a case. This is where you find out what they have and give them all you have; however, the best attitude to have here is that you now have the power to make them see the whole case. But also, you have the ability to see exactly what angle they are taking against you so you can prepare battle with that in mind.

The judge will issue you a time frame to have the discovery done and he will describe the method to have it completed. For the most part a case is given thirty (30) interrogatories, thirty (30) requests for production of documents and (30) requests for admissions.

Interrogatories are questions that you send to the Agency (the attorney appointed to the case) then he will search out the answers and return to you and vice versa. You will be able to send 30 questions (to include subparts). Subparts are the secondary questions within a question. For example:

What was said to the Postmaster concerning the complainant? Include the following:

- *Date*
- *Who said it*
- *In what tone was it stated*

That is a question with subparts. However, rather than break down a question be creative and make it one question without subparts such as:

- *Specify with clarity what discussions the Postmaster had concerning the complainant from May 14, 2007 through June 1, 2007*

Remember the basic rule in interrogatories—Never ask a question that you don't already know the answer to! Your purpose is to make the agency see YOUR point of view so ask questions that support your view and get them to state it on paper.

For example if the case has sexual harassment in it and you know you are innocent and there was never any investigations nor discussions concerning it until they used it as a "mere pretext" for their actions then ask:

- *Declare with specifics and clarity as to the comments made, physical contact initiated, and to whom they were direct to with support from documentation of any investigation, discussions or discipline prior to this complaint performed by management upon the complainant.*

A request for production of documentation is when you request the document that they talk about or indicate in the affidavits completed during the formal investigation. You want proof. You want the document spoken of or referred to that is otherwise not provided.

A request for admission is when you absolutely want clarification from a statement in an affidavit claiming a fact in a round about way, indirectly. You place a request for admission with wording that cannot be misconstrued if the case goes to civil court.

Depositions are performed with a court reporter and the persons being deposed attorney present. The party doing the deposing pays for the court reporter and the transcript of the deposition. If the complainant deposes anyone that is a federal employee the agency MUST make the employee available for the deposition. If they are not a federal employee then it is the cost of the party doing the deposing to make arrangements with the witness.

The remainder of the Order will brief you on any/all reasons the judge may decide to throw out the case or deny actions for such violations of the 29 C.F.R. & 1614.606. I cannot elaborate or plead enough on the importance of your reading this Order per each word, sentence and meaning. If you are smart and have retained an attorney then you don't need to worry about it—it is his/her responsibility and they are trained for such.

You will be notified of whom the representative for the Agency is and again, please do not get in a hurry. I received my documentation from the judge on February 8th, 2007 and I received the declaration of representation (the name of the attorney) on February 23rd, 2008. They had 3 weeks from the date of the Acknowledgement and Order (Feb 7, 2008) to attempt a resolution, as ordered by the judge; however, they wasted 2 of those weeks before assigning it to an attorney and they never once offered an attempt by the end of the 3 weeks. On the other hand, I had submitted an attempt of resolution, sent in my request for production of documents and my interrogatories to the manager of the USPS law dept before they had any one assigned to it.

You will receive from their attorney (ies) a request for documents, interrogatories and most generally a date for deposition. You can do depositions also; however, keep in mind, that the cost of the court reporter and transferring into a transcript is YOUR cost. You can avoid this cost by getting consent from their attorney (ies) to allow you to provide questionnaires to those you intend to have as a witness. It will save the company money in down time and production loss; however, they are not obligated to do so. In my case, they denied the consent. Their reason was that I wasn't on issue. That was their attempt to manipulate and intimidate me.

Each judge will determine how long you have for which juncture in the case.

Mine was:

➢ Provide designation of representation within 14 calendar days
➢ 21 calendar days to attempt resolution
➢ Discovery shall be completed within 65 calendar days
➢ Discovery must be initiated within 30 calendar days
➢ Parties must respond to a request for discovery within 30 calendar days from receipt of request
➢ Motions must be filed within ten calendar days
➢ Opposing statements against the motions must be filed within ten calendar days of receipt of motion

- ➢ A motion for summary judgment must be filed within 75 calendar days
- ➢ Opposing party must respond to motion for summary within 15 calendar days
- ➢ Moving party will then have 5 calendar days to file a response to the opposition

Notice the CALENDAR DAYS? Everything associated with the EEO complaint process is in calendar days. These are in calendar days from the date of the Acknowledgement and Scheduling Order dated February 7, 2008.

Do not be shocked if the Agency submits a request for Summary of Judgment. It is a process they attempt to manipulate the system and persuade the judge to rule quickly without a trial while claiming you have no case. It will have statements twisted and out of context; however, the unknowing will believe them to be true. Hence, you should not hesitate to provide your response to dispel their request. You will have 10 days to respond and then they will be given 5 days to respond against your response to their request. The exact time frames will be provided within your Schedule and Acknowledgment Order.

It was during the discovery process for my latest case that I came to believe the EEOC Judge was very prejudice in favor of the Postal Service, thus, I decided to withdraw my request for a hearing within the EEO channels. Reason of thought was based on that I had filed a Motion to compel when the Agency interviewed several employees; yet, had denied me the same opportunity (unless I allowed them to help configure my questions). The Judge had ruled it appropriate for the Agency to have the right to interview and depose; yet, being the Complainant, I was allowed only the right to depose. He additionally stated that if I had not the financial resources to do depositions then he suggested that I take this process to the Federal court and have an attorney appointed to the case.

So to bypass this (in my opinion) bias judge, I submitted a withdrawal of my request for a hearing and requested a Final Agency Decision.

The logic to this was to take the legal judgment from, what I considered, a bias judge and place it back into the Postal Service management's decision.

Therefore, I could appeal it to the EEOC in Washington DC for a legal opinion in a shorter timeframe than pursuing it through the hearing avenue. Thereby, I shortened the time to getting my case into Federal Civil court.

If you continue with the hearing procedures you will be required to provide the ***Pre-hearing submissions*** as instructed in the court order. Read yours thoroughly, as it will direct you on exactly what the judge has so ordered to be included and when it is determined to be submitted.

You will be given a ***Pre-hearing Conference*** (most probable via a three-way phone conference). This will be further instructed within your court order and you will receive—or should receive—a written communication prior to the conference providing you with exacts of day, time, issues and who will be included in the conference. You will be provided the opportunity to state your case and hear what the Agencies counsel will argue. Do not get argumentative or unruly—that does not bid well for you. If you have a representative be sure he/she fully understands what you expect and will accept for terms of resolution before you start this meeting. It is not common for resolutions to be arrived at during this stage so do not anticipate such happening.

At your ***Hearing*** you should have an attorney or a very well specialized representative. The agency will be fully represented by their law department. Each case is different so I will not delve into this aspect; except, to repeat myself in suggesting you have an attorney.

If you requested a Final Agency Decision rather than a hearing, then they will have 40 days from the date of your request to issue you a reply (unless you requested your Final Agency Decision after you have already participated in or currently were participating in a court proceeding). On my latest EEO complaint the judge ruled a Dismissal and gave the Agency 60 days after receipt of the order to provide a decision.

Appendix 1
Timelines
_____

All days are considered CALENDAR days

Initiating the complaint:

- *45 days* from alleged discriminatory action

Or

- *45 days* of effective date of personnel action

Initial Pre-complaint Form 2564-A:

- *10 days* after you received them.

DRS Counseling:

- *30 days*—from initial date you contact the EEO complaint center
- *60 days*—if you agree to sign a 2567-A allowing extended time
- *90 days*—if you agree to participate in REDRESS

Initiate a Formal Complaint:

- *15 days* after you receive the PS Form 2579, Notice of Right to File.

Formal Investigation Period:

- *180 days* of date the complaint was filed
- *270 days* if you and the Postal Service agree in writing to extend the time

- *360 days* if you amend the case while it is in the formal investigation stage
- *360 days* if you have more than one complaint consolidated for investigation

Requesting a Final Decision or an EEOC Hearing:

- *30 days* from the date you receive the investigative file

Be sure to send a copy of your request for either a hearing or decision to BOTH the EEOC district office AND the NEEOISO office at the same time—these addresses will be included in the letter you receive along with the investigation file

Actions after Acknowledgment but before the Hearing:

- *14 days* to provide the administrative judge and opposing party a copy of the Designation of Representative.
- *21 days* to contact opposing party to initiate resolution attempts
- *30 days* to initiate discovery
- *65 days* to complete discovery
- *75 days* to file the Pre-hearing Submissions

Notice of Final Action and Appeal rights:

- *40 days* from date of Postal Services receipt of the administrative judge's decision or your request for a Final Agency Decision.

Appealing the Dismissal or a Decision:

30 days of receipt of:

- Dismissal for Investigation
- Postal Service Final Action
- Administrative Judges Decision—(If the Postal Service fails to issue you a final action within 40 days—you may file an appeal to this decision within the 30 days from the expiration of the 40 day period.
- Merit Final Agency Decision

Be sure to send a copy of your appeal to **BOTH** the **EEOC** district office AND the **NEEOISO** office at the same time—these addresses will be included in the letter you receive along with the investigation file

Filing a Civil Action:

- *90 days* of receipt of decision or final action (providing you have not appealed).
- *90 days* after you receive the OFO's final decision on appeal.
- *180 days* from date of filing the formal complaint if no final action has been issued by Postal Service from administrative judge's decision or a final agency decision.
- *180 days* from date of filing the appeal with OFO if no final decision has been issued.

www.ingramcontent.com/pod-product-compliance
Lightning Source LLC
Chambersburg PA
CBHW031331290526
45784CB00014B/2550